BRITAIN IN OLD PH

AROUND CROMER

MARTIN WARREN

ALAN SUTTON PUBLISHING LIMITED

Alan Sutton Publishing Limited
Phoenix Mill · Far Thrupp · Stroud
Gloucestershire · GL5 2BU

First published 1995

Front cover photograph: East Beach, *c.* 1895.
Back cover photograph: Cromer fishermen saluting Mrs Buxton, probably 1929.

British Library Cataloguing in Publication Data.
A catalogue record for this book is available from the British Library.

ISBN 0–7509–0787–8

Typeset in 9/10 Sabon.
Typesetting and origination by
Alan Sutton Publishing Limited.
Printed in Great Britain by
Hartnolls, Bodmin, Cornwall.

For Stefanija

Contents

Railway poster, late 1930s. 'Come to Cromer Where the Poppies grow'. Designed by Bruce Angrave for the London and North Eastern and London, Midland and Scottish Railways.

Introduction

Daniel Defoe wrote, in the eighteenth century, that he knew nothing Cromer was famous for except lobsters and being the terror of sailors (they called it the Devil's Throat). The busy sea trade around the Norfolk coast brought many fatalities when ships ran aground on sand banks or ran ashore in storms. This led to one of the first lifeboats being stationed at Cromer in 1804. The exploits of the Cromer lifeboat are famous and Henry Blogg, who was coxswain through two world wars, is the most highly decorated of lifeboatmen ever. The crew is, and always has been, largely drawn from fishermen. This community within a community fishes from the open beaches within a few miles of the town. Cromer crabs and lobsters have been caught here for centuries, using traditional double-ended wooden crab boats and home-made hoop-nets and crab pots. Though rarely large, the Cromer crabs are renowned for their quality and flavour.

Cromer's early visitors were mainly gentry and professional people from the county. There were no public rooms, so Cromer attracted people of retiring habits who enjoyed nature and scenery rather than sociability. In the latter part of the eighteenth century a number of families (particularly the inter-related Gurneys, Barclays and Hoares) began to take regular holidays in lodgings here. Eventually they bought land and built property. They enjoyed shooting, riding on the sands and sea-bathing. Cromer gained a reputation as a select bathing place, and by the 1840s the directories were describing it as a 'fashionable watering place'.

Railways did not reach Cromer until 1877. Even then the station was a mile out of town. It was another ten years before the railway was extended into the town and the Beach station was built. Cromer developed rapidly in the next decade, seized by an entrepreneurial fervour. By the turn of the century the place had more or less acquired its modern appearance, with a new promenade, pier, grand hotels and rapidly growing suburbs. The Council was eager to maintain the select character of the town. They ensured Cromer had gas and electricity; they installed waterworks and sewerage schemes and widened roads. The holiday trade reached its zenith before the First World War, but throughout this century Cromer has continued to expand as a residential town.

Some of the images of Cromer included within this volume date from before 1851, barely a decade after the invention of photography. By the 1860s the fashionable watering place had two commercial photographers: Tom Morley was a tobacconist and hairdresser in Garden Street; David Savin was a watchmaker and cutter of jet and amber. The latter started in one room and later moved to 23 Church Street. Tom Mack succeeded Tom Morley in business and later moved next to Savin. Several of their early views of the town have survived, including some superb glass plates by Savin.

Herbert Mace had a caravan studio on the beach. In the late 1880s he also had a camera obscura, which was a great novelty in the days before moving pictures. It consisted of an octagonal wooden shed with a revolving lens on the top. Inside, a moving, colour image of the whole beach was projected on to a tabletop screen. He also had a photographic studio on the corner of Garden Street and Corner Street. Later he went into partnership with Thomas Mase of Norwich and moved into Balcony House on the corner of Mount Street and Church Street. Augustus Mace had a studio at 25 Garden Street in 1899. On the edge of town Walter Royall had a glass lean-to photographic studio in the former stonemason's yard, opposite Chesterfield Villas, West Street.

Daniel Davison ran a pharmacy in Jetty Street but was also an enthusiastic recorder of the new seaside resort, though he was no great artist or technician. He left us many glass plates from late Victorian and Edwardian Cromer and several of his pictures appeared in the early guide books and promotions. London portrait photographer Olive Edis and her sister Katherine had a studio at the bottom of the Gangway in the early 1900s. Though Olive specialized in high society, she did some wonderful studies of the Cromer and Sheringham fishermen. In 1912 A.J. Rogers had a studio in Church Street in the arcade now occupied by the Midland Bank. Harry H. Tansley succeeded him, between the wars, and worked into the 1950s at Sheringham as well as Cromer. He was about the only photographer operating in the town during the Second World War.

Commercial photographers such as Francis Frith, Poulton and Jarrold and Sons published crisp sepia-toned prints of the town and its environs. They were sold in sets and in frames and many of these have survived, though they are often faded now. Naturally thousands of postcards were published too, both by local photographers and national firms.

Walter Rye, the Victorian historian, wrote the most authoritative account of the early history of Cromer. The first systematic modern history was published in 1936 by Alfred C. Savin, son of David the photographer. Londoner Cyril Crawford Holden settled in the town and spent the years until he died, in 1976, passionately collecting pictures and prints, maps, notes, reminiscences and anecdotes. We are greatly indebted to his efforts as they form the cornerstone of the Cromer Museum's local history collection: many of the pictures reproduced here are from his collection. Most importantly, he meticulously researched and recorded the details of those pictures – names, businesses, dates, events, etc. The space available in this volume is too small to do justice to what we know about the pictures. For further information you should visit the museum. The collection is a rich one and forms an invaluable archive of the changing town. We are always keen to add new pictures, especially unpublished ones, very early ones and records of twentieth-century life.

Section One

THE OLD TOWN

'Cromer is a fashionable bathing place and well-built town, picturesquely seated on the lofty sea cliffs, at the most north-east point of the Norfolk Coast. . . . The number of visitors continues to increase yearly and for the accommodation of this growing influx of company, many neat houses have been erected during the last 40 years.'

White's Directory, *1845.*

St Peter and St Paul's Church after the renovation of the tower, 1885. The chancel was restored in 1887. Church Street was widened by an average of 12ft at this time and part of the churchyard was paved. There is an inscription to that effect on the wall today.

The church is large for the size of the town and was built in the perpendicular style of the late fourteenth and early fifteenth century. It owes much to the liberality of the local ship owners and merchants. In the seventeenth century the condition of the church declined, and the chancel was so ruinous that the Revd Thomas Gill sought to pull it down in 1681 to save the cost of rebuilding. Tradition has it that he used gunpowder, leaving only one fragment of the arcade remaining.

Until the Great Eastern Railway reached Cromer, in 1877, it was just a cluster of houses and cottages around the church, with scattered residences and farms. This view, from the Cromer High station at the top of Norwich Road, shows just how small the town was in 1880.

View from East Cliff, 1864–7. In the foreground the ladies are sitting at the top of Doctor's Steps, named after Dr Sidney Terry of nearby Cliff House. Note the houses on the Crescent have only two storeys (see p. 18).

The Loke, 1880s. Church Street was not fully developed until this time. This view looks down the lower part of the Loke, now Hans Place. The Regal Cinema (opened in July 1914 by Edward Troller) now stands on the left. R.A. Clarke's tiny lock-up butcher's is on the right of the lane.

The Lord Nelson Coffee Tavern, pre-1891. This was the centre of the temperance movement in Cromer and was run from 1880 to 1891. The site is now the junction of Mount Street with Church Street, where traffic thunders around the corner of Balcony House. Note the painting of the Norfolk hero on the roof.

Church Street, *c.* 1875. A little girl stands on flint cobbles in Church Street and looks into the window of Miss Cubitt's Shell Shop. Back in the 1830s this cottage was occupied by Thomas Leak, chemist and stationer; he also ran a library and, later, his daughter Mary had a School of Young Ladies; another daughter ran a millinery and corset business here. In 1878 the premises were pulled down and 36–8 Church Street or Vernon House was built.

Ditchell's house and barn in Tucker Street, 1800s. Anthony Ditchell was a merchant in the eighteenth century and behind his barn was a steep wooden runway for taking goods from the ships on the beach straight into it. Both barn and house were demolished in 1893 when the Hotel Metropole was built.

West Street, 1893. All these buildings, except the White Horse Inn (behind the distant figures), have been demolished. On the left is Mr Golden, blacksmith, then Henry Amis and his family outside their greengrocery and fishmongers' shop. The two boys across the street are the boot repairer's children – 'Skinney' and 'Hardtimes' Plumley.

David Dulley's chemist shop, 1899. The man on the left in the shop doorway is probably David Dulley, who had taken over the business from the late Mr Priest. A delivery boy with his basket is in the alleyway. This building is still a chemist's shop in 1995.

High Street, almost 2 o'clock by the church clock, 7 September 1886. You can see just what the surface of the street was like before the metalling of the 1890s; a mixture of sand, gravel and beach pebbles – and a liberal sprinkling of horse dung. William Murrell's shop sign, at the right, is advertising close and open carriages, dog carts, omnibus and gig conveyances, etc. On the left is the back entrance to the Hotel de Paris, a boot and shoe repairer's and two millinery shops.

Prospect House (on the corner) and Woodbine Cottages, West Street, seen here shortly before these properties were demolished in 1910 to make way for the new Methodist chapel. Those were the days when you could walk in the middle of the road. Prospect House was owned in around 1887 by Mrs Rogers, and later occupied by Charles Smith, barman of the Ship Hotel and father of the confectioner Percy Smith.

Fountain House, *c.* 1870. In front of it is the town pump. Chapel Street or Pump Street is to the left. The Cromer Urban District Council offices were here from 1900 to 1925.

View from Garden Street of the garden and back of Hanover House, probably 1890s. Perhaps the most ancient house in Cromer, its characteristic gable appears as a conspicuous feature in the earliest image of the town, an early eighteenth-century painting that hangs in nearby Felbrigg Hall. Though the gable is simpler now, visitors to Budgens' car park may recognize the door and flint cottage.

Church Street, 1880s. On the extreme left is Tom Mack's: he was photographer and optician, lapidarist, jet and ornament dealer. Next to him is D.W. Savin, photographer, fancy jewellery and antique dealer. On the right is Claremont House, faced with pebbles selected from the beach: it was demolished in 1901 to make way for the Baptist church.

Church Street, *c.* 1901. A policeman is on duty outside the Albion Hotel. On the right is Beech House, owned by the Sandford family, who were farmers, boat owners and auctioneers. The house was demolished to make way for the new building now occupied by the Eastern Electricity showrooms.

The Gangway, 1875. This shows it before it was paved with granite sets. The skyline of Brunswick House (centre) and Brunswick Terrace beyond is remarkably unaltered but the houses on the Crescent have a third storey added (see page 9). On the beach (right) is what appears to be the remains of a house for a windlass. At the top of Gangway, with the placard 'Du Cann' across the doors, is the lifeboat house and fishermen's look-out room, with its library above it. The lifeboat house, with the turret, was built in 1867 to house the *Benjamin Bond Cabbell,* but was replaced when the larger *Louisa Heartwell* came in 1902.

Section Two

CROMER CRABS

'Cromer crabs' is the name given to the real Cromer people as well as being delicious shellfish from north Norfolk. The people are typified by the fishing families who inhabited the yards and cottages in the centre of the town. These fishermen are launching their boat to go to inspect their pots.

Crab boats and hovellers, East Runton Gap, August 1888. This must be an almost timeless scene on the north Norfolk coast. For centuries fishermen exploited these natural gaps to carry their lightly built crab boats out of the way of the tide. The crab pots were introduced from Yorkshire around 1863 and revolutionized the catching of crabs. Also visible here are longshore drift nets, tows, anchors and bait.

Preparing for the start of the season, early 1900s. Fishermen on the East Beach are loading up their boats, ready to take the pots to sea. In those days each crab pot was separate, with its own marker or dan buoy. It was known as a 'swummer'. Today the pots are roped together in 'shanks' of twenty or twenty-five and marked with buoys at each end.

Launching a crab boat, early 1900s. This was almost as hazardous as coming ashore. One of the fishermen had to keep the boat headed into the waves or they could easily be capsized. Once beyond the breakers they could use their single dipping lugsail to reach the pots if need be.

West Beach fisherman 'Wessun' Allen hauling crab pots the hard way, early 1900s.

'Wessun' Allen baiting up the long lines with whelks, *c.* 1909. Many hundreds of hooks had to be baited before they set to sea. On the left is 'Sailor' Allen.

Hauling crabs by hand, *c.* 1950. This arduous way of earning a living meant aching backs and hands blistered and covered in seawater boils. George Cully (left) of East Runton baits the pots aboard his boat *Myosotis* while Peter Mayes of Suffield Park, Cromer hauls. Today all boats are fitted with hydraulic haulers. These take a great deal of the strain and allow one boat to fish more pots.

Launching 'Tuna' Harrison's motor crab boat *Ever Hopeful* in the 1950s. On board are 'Stymie' Blyth (port oar), 'Dick' Davies (starboard oar), 'Tuna' Harrison (climbing in the stern). Peter Mayes is at the port quarter and 'Buster' Grout is pushing hard.

The Gangway, *c.* 1946. The fishermen are mending their pots, at the end of the season, ready to store them for the winter. The larger pots are for lobsters. Left to right: Leslie 'Tater' Harrison, Kelly Harrison (Leslie's eldest son), Bob Davies, Dereck Harrison (toddler son of Kelly), 'Yacker' Harrison (Leslie's second son), 'Tuna' Harrison (Leslie's youngest son), Frank Davies (drowned in *Boy Jimmy* in 1953), George Rook (down slope), 'Elmo' Flaxman.

Fishermen usually made their own crab pots. Traditionally the pots had an oak-framed base with a heavy iron bottom called a 'music' because it resembled an instrument keyboard. The hoops and bars were of hazel, cut from the local hedgerows, and the net was braided from manila hemp, or 'pot stuff'.

Fisherman and lifeboatman Charlie Cox in his crab boat *White Heather*, *c.* 1925. He and his brother-in-law, Gilbert Mayes, owned the boat jointly. He displays one of the Cromer crabs as he packs them into his ped (basket). Crabs were often sent alive to market by train.

Portrait of a fishing family, 1934. Charlie Cox is shown with his wife Emma (right), daughter Mabel March and grandchildren Richard and Jean. Within a week Charlie was dead, drowned with Gilbert Mayes when *White Heather* capsized on 28 July 1934. His funeral procession was half a mile long and attended by fishermen and lifeboatmen from all along the Norfolk coast.

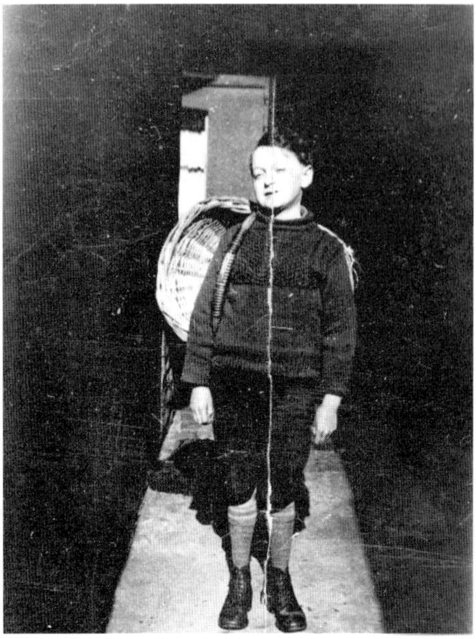

All the bloaters sold. Ten-year-old Don Cox stands, with his empty basket, in the alleyway of the family fish shop, wearing his home-knitted gansey, 1928. Don and his twin brother Harry were the last to use a sailing crab boat at Cromer, the *Viking*, in 1962. Don later became a coastguard at Mundesley.

Fishermen's cottages off Surrey Street (alias Gooseberry Lane), *c.* 1960. These cottages have now been demolished. Note the dan buoys, made of cork floats, hanging on the wall.

Cromer fishermen posing for the *Daily Herald* photographer and cheering Mrs Buxton. This may be the election of 1929 when her husband, Noel Buxton, became the Labour MP. Waving their caps, left to right: 'Ponsey' Harrison, -?- , Charlie Brackenbury, -?-, Charlie Cox (see p. 25), -?-, -?-, 'Bluker' Stimpson, Walter 'Primo' Allen, George Cox (who owned the crab boat *Don't Know*, YH 31, built in 1924), Ted Cook.

Mrs Faith Davies' crab stall on the corner of Church Street and Gangway, 1935. Faith was married to William ('Billy') Davies, see p. 29. Mrs Ellen Wright of Leicester is buying a crab from Mrs Davies at Whitsuntide. The building is an eighteenth-century granary which was converted to cottages in the earlier part of the nineteenth century for the benefit of the coastguards. The Davies family still has a stall here today.

John James Davies' family, *c.* 1909. Back row, left to right: William T. Davies, Kitty, Jack, Henry Blogg, his wife Annie. Front row, left to right: Nancy Davies, Beatrice, John James Davies, Martha Davies holding baby Queenie (Henry and Annie's daughter). J.J. Davies had retired as lifeboat coxswain in 1902. His stepson, Henry Blogg, was destined to become famous as the lifeboat coxswain.

Fisherman George 'Skinback' Cox carrying a crab boat sail along the Narrows in Church Street. George was Charlie Cox's brother, see p. 25.

The yacht *Agnes Etta* with her crew of fishermen and a family of summer visitors (the Lancasters?) below the Bath Hotel, 1880s. The *Agnes Etta* was one of two boats used by the Kirby family for visitors' pleasure trips. The men in the boat are, left to right: Bob Warner, Jimmy 'Buttons' Harrison (standing tallest behind), George 'Stag' Kirby, William 'Hackering' Kirby (seated: he was a sailmaker), Tom 'Bentley' Kirby and 'Dirty' George Kirby. This comes from one of many glass plates discovered in 1966 in the attic of Herbert Mace's old studio at Balcony House, on the corner of Mount Street and Church Street. Unfortunately many were broken beyond repair but enough of this one survived to be reproduced here.

Section Three

MARITIME

'"Ready to die" is the motto of men – and this is the reason the lifeboat's manned.'

Clement Scott.

The coal ship *Wensleydale*, 1872. The crew would lay a kedge anchor and hawser astern as she came ashore on the high tide. Once unloaded they would haul on the anchor to get off again. On the right, the Bath Hotel is being extended. The spoil from the excavations has been unceremoniously dumped over the seawall.

A rare event of three coal ships on the beach at once, 1868. *Wensleydale*, on the left, was owned by Jeremiah Cross of Overstrand, who had coal yards in Surrey Street and Brook Street. In the centre is *Commerce* belonging to the Sandford family, whose yard was at the top of Gangway. The yard later became the East Coast Motor Company. On the right is *Ellis* owned by Nathaniel Field of East Runton.

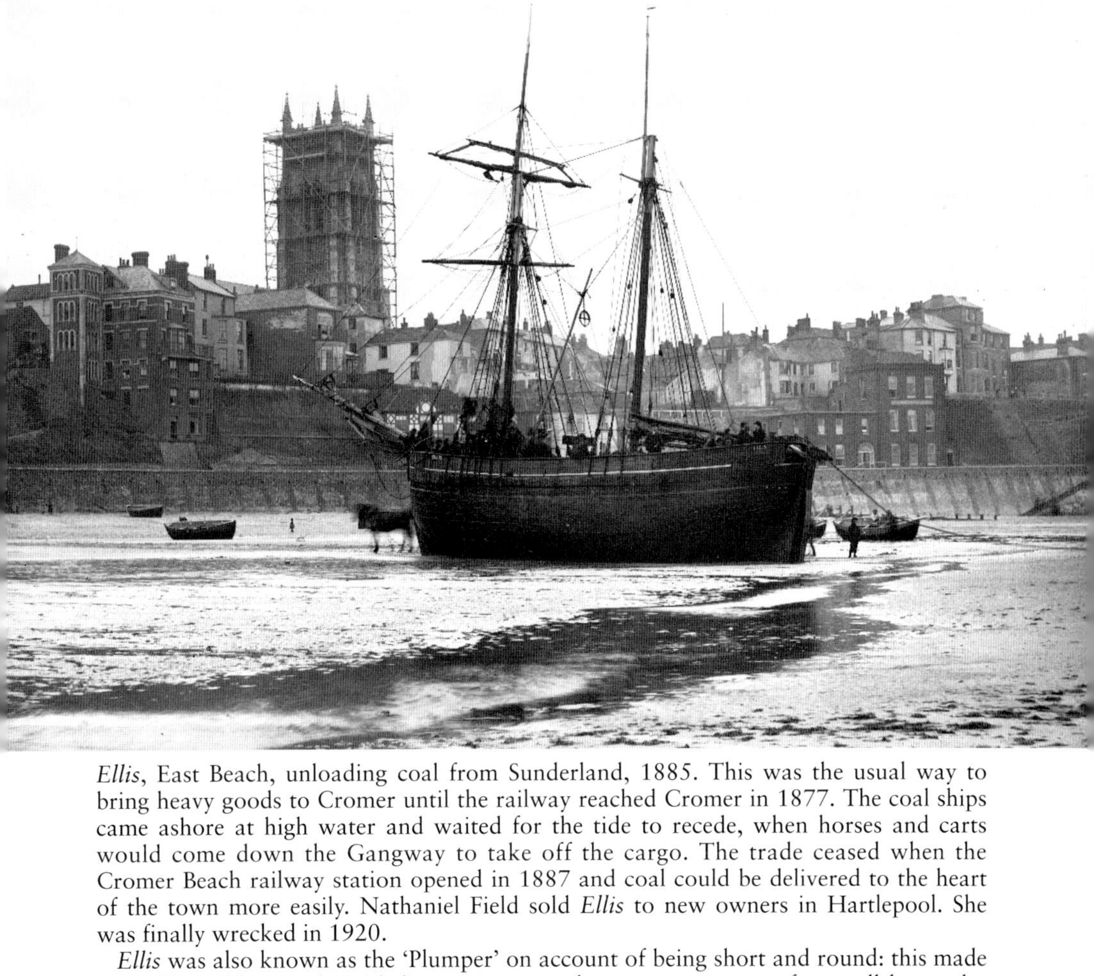

Ellis, East Beach, unloading coal from Sunderland, 1885. This was the usual way to bring heavy goods to Cromer until the railway reached Cromer in 1877. The coal ships came ashore at high water and waited for the tide to recede, when horses and carts would come down the Gangway to take off the cargo. The trade ceased when the Cromer Beach railway station opened in 1887 and coal could be delivered to the heart of the town more easily. Nathaniel Field sold *Ellis* to new owners in Hartlepool. She was finally wrecked in 1920.

Ellis was also known as the 'Plumper' on account of being short and round: this made her roll terribly. People said that a voyage on her was a sure cure for small boys who wanted to go to sea. In the background is a wonderful piece of wooden scaffolding, erected for the renovation of the church tower.

Coastguards, Old Coastguard Station (now Watch House), 1870. Their naval-style uniform with muskets and leather hats reminds us that the early work of the coastguard was to do with the prevention of smuggling and acting as a naval reserve. The men lived in cottages at the top of the Gangway, the Commander (right) at Newstead House.

Cromer Lighthouse and Keeper's Cottage, 1890s. The lighthouse was built in 1833 to replace an earlier one that was threatened by cliff erosion. At first it was lit by oil lamps, later converted to town gas and, in 1936, to electricity. It is now fully automated and the beam can be seen from 21 miles away.

Coastguard station, Marrams, Runton Road, *c.* 1945. The station moved here in 1927. Coastguard duties by that time had become mostly safety at sea and coordination of rescue; they continue so today. Left to right: A.H. Bennett, Station Officer Purdy, -?-, District Officer Sworn, -?-, Patrick MacDonald, Jack Marjoram.

A coastguard exercise at Weybourne using the breeches buoy, *c.* 1947. The victim in the buoy is No. 2 auxiliary coastguard and lifeboat launcher 'Friday' Balls; in the foreground, standing, left to right: -?-, 'Ginger' Rogers, Bobby Briggs (No. 1 auxiliary coastguard and jeweller), -?-, Commander Bill Whiting (in peaked cap), Bill Platten, ? Scott.

The wreck of the 200-ton brigantine *Agenoria* on the beach below the Gangway, 9 April 1868. This illustrates the fate of so many ships which have foundered while attempting to round Cromer. The combination of treacherous offshore sand banks and a long, curving coastline with few harbours earned this stretch of sea the name the 'Devil's Throat'. After one tide the *Agenoria* became a total wreck. Scenes like this led to the establishment of a lifeboat station at Cromer as early as 1804.

The wreck of the *Alpha*, between Cromer and East Runton, October 1883. The Cromer lifeboat crew couldn't launch the *Benjamin Bond Cabbell* into the strong wind and heavy sea. Following an enquiry they changed the lifeboat to a lighter non-self-righter preferred by the fishermen.

Cromer No. 2 lifeboat *Alexandria* in action on the *Sepoy* in December 1933. In atrocious conditions, despite valiant efforts, the lifeboat could not effect a rescue. When the No. 1 boat returned from service elsewhere, Henry Blogg and his crew carried out one of the bravest of manoeuvres – that of driving the boat repeatedly on to the decks – to take the crew off.

The wreck of the *Esras*, 21 March 1901. The crew and helpers are moving the lifeboat *Benjamin Bond Cabbell II* along the promenade to launch it from the West Beach and so avoid hitting the pier. They managed to get the boat over the seawall and on to the beach with a great deal of trouble. The lifeboat was unable to launch into the heavy surf before, at the fifth attempt, the Cromer and Sheringham Rocket Brigade managed to get a line to the stricken vessel. All the crew were rescued by breeches buoy by the Rocket Brigade.

An illustration by Lancelot Speed from the *Sphere* magazine, dramatizing the scene depicted opposite.

The Greek steamer *Pyrin*, 9 January 1917. A perilous day: two ships were wrecked off Cromer and Cromer lifeboat had a busy time. Here *Pyrin* is aground below the lighthouse. Her crew of sixteen was rescued by the lifeboat *Louisa Heartwell*. The wreck is under military guard, perhaps to discourage looting.

Later the same afternoon the Swedish steamer *Fernebo* was driven ashore after being slit in two when her boilers exploded. Behind her the *Pyrin* is already ashore. The heroic rescue of all members of both crews is a stirring tale too long to recount here. Only one man died, lost in the explosion on board the second ship. For the tenacity which made them work well into the night the lifeboat crew received many awards, and Coxswain Blogg received the gold medal of the RNLI.

Launching ceremony of the *H.F. Bailey*, 26 July 1923. Coxswain Henry Blogg and Lady Frances Suffield are at the launching ceremony of Cromer's first motor lifeboat. The boathouse at the end of the pier still serves as the lifeboat station today.

Cromer lifeboat, the fourth to be called *H.F. Bailey*, *c.* 1945.

Opposite above:
Police Inspector Balls takes 'Monte' into quarantine, 1932. On 16 October 1932, the Cromer lifeboat saved twenty-nine of the crew of the *Monte Novoso* and took them to Gorleston. The next day Henry Blogg and his crew returned to the ship and found that the captain and the three officers, who had elected to remain with the ship, had been taken off by a small boat. Blogg heard some dogs barking and Jack Davies (see page 29) and others went on board. One dog rushed out in fright and fell into the sea but behind another door stood a large St Bernard. They brought it on board the lifeboat, together with some caged birds, and returned to Cromer. Captain Solvature Angelivo gave Monte to Blogg and it remained his close companion until it died in 1935.

Opposite below:
The crew of the Spanish government ship *Cantabria* with the lifeboat crew that rescued them, 1938. The *Cantabria* was attacked by the Spanish nationalist gunboat *Nadar*. Left to right: Jack Davies, Henry Blogg, Frank Davies (behind), the skipper of the *Cantabria*, Faith Davies (behind), -?- (obscured), wife of Spanish skipper, Jimmy Davies, George 'Bluker' Stimpson, a Spanish crew member, Bob Davies. The Spanish skipper's two children are in front.

Cromer lifeboat crew in front of the *H.F. Bailey* on the end of the pier, 1932. Left to right: Robert Davies (engineer), Bob 'Young Dinger' Blogg, Billy 'Pimpo' Davies (killed at Cromer in a bombing raid, July 1942), Jack Davies (father of Billy 'Pimpo'), Walter 'Primo' Allen (signalman: he died, aged forty-nine, of exposure after being washed overboard during the rescue of forty-four men from the merchant ship *English Trader*, 26 October 1941), Gilbert Mayes (drowned 12 July 1932 in crab boat *White Heather*), Frank Davies (Billy's son), Henry Blogg (coxswain), Jimmy Davies, Jack Davies Jnr, George Cox ('Skinback' Cox's son, see p. 29), Arthur 'Cutler' Balls, George 'Buckram' Balls, Charlie Cox (drowned with Gilbert Mayes in *White Heather,* see p. 25).

Section Four

ROAD & RAIL

Great Eastern Railway, Cromer High station, c. 1904. On the left is an 0–6–0 tank engine, on the right a T19 class locomotive (number 768) leaving for Norwich. The lack of a railway inhibited the growth of Cromer, as it could only be reached by coach or by sea. This suited some parties, who preferred Cromer unspoilt, but the businessmen saw a coast ripe for exploitation.

Driver Robert Pygle of Holt leans on the shaft of the Norwich coach, Tucker Street, *c.* 1894. On the left is Tucker's Hotel, built in the early 1800s, one of the first in Cromer. The Metropole (centre) was one of a spate of hotels built in the boom of the early 1890s and, like many, it was designed by the Norwich architect George Skipper. In the foreground are the gravestones on the north side of the churchyard of St Peter and St Paul. One gravestone was removed when the street was widened.

Thomas Cook's 'Lobster Coach', *c.* 1909, so-called because it carried fresh lobsters from Cromer to Norwich. By this time the day trip from the Grand Hotel, Cromer to Norwich and back was something of a novelty. The fare was 10*s* single, 12*s* 6*d* return and the journey took two and a half hours. The horses were changed at Roughton, Aylsham and Newton St Faith's, and the coach stopped for tea at Aylsham on the return.

An unusual snapshot from the window of a charabanc or omnibus as it stands in High Street, Overstrand. The carriage on the right is waiting to take passengers into Cromer. None of the land on the right has yet been developed.

Cromer High station, 1877. The first railway station to open at Cromer, this was located at the top of the Norwich road a mile from the beach. The arrival of the East Norfolk Railway, later the Great Eastern, was an important step in opening up the seaside trade at Cromer. The trains could boast a journey time from London of 2 hours 55 minutes.

The High station, 1962. Cromer's railway network had been considerably altered in recent years, principally by the closures of the Cromer to Mundesley line in 1953 and Cromer High station in 1954. The British Transport Commission decided that having two stations in Cromer was not economical, although High station continued to handle goods until 1959.

Cromer Beach station, shortly after it opened, 1887. This belonged to the Eastern and Midlands Railway (later Midland and Great Northern), providing the direct route between 'Poppyland' and the Midlands and north of England. The train waiting at the platform is headed by a Beyer Peacock 4–4–0 locomotive, no. 25.

Cromer Beach station, in 1914, when traffic was at its peak. The left of the picture is now the site of Safeway's supermarket, and at the time of writing a new use is being sought for the station buildings.

A 4–4–0 Lord Claude Hamilton-class locomotive, named after the chairman of the Great Eastern Railway, leaving Cromer High. Precise dating is not possible, but this probably pre-dates the amalgamation of the Great Eastern Railway with the London and North Eastern Railway in 1923.

Queen Alexandra alighting from a carriage at Cromer High, 1902. She had been visiting Lord Hillingdon at Overstrand.

Staff of the Great Eastern Railway, Cromer High, 1910. Among them, on the middle row, are Charlie Laycock (second from the left), ? Hannant (third from the left), Victor Laycock (seventh from the left), Oswald Cook, (seventh from the right), delivery driver 'Jumbo' Lambert (far right). Fourth from the left in the front row is ? Arbon.

Inspector Oswald Cook in the uniform of the Great Eastern Railway, *c.* 1910.

The branch line from Cromer Beach station, early 1900s. It runs through a cutting and out past the works of the Cromer Gas Company to the west of Howard's Hill. Coal had to be brought by rail and, in 1875, gas was first made in Mill Road close to the Cromer High Station. The first street lighting – lit by gas, of course – came to Station Road in 1885. The larger gasworks (seen here) were needed to supply the progressive town and they opened in 1900. Anglian Water redeveloped the gas works site as a sewage treatment works in 1993–4.

Ted Balls (left) and his conductor, *c.* 1920. He drove this bus for the United Bus Company on the Norwich–Aylsham, Roughton and Cromer route. The vehicle was the first in the area and was an AEC 'Y' type converted from an ex-War Department army lorry.

A charabanc excursion to Aylmerton, *c.* 1900. Many of the village churches in the area have round towers which date back to the Saxon and Norman periods. Their round shape probably results from the difficulty of making corners from flint, the local building stone.

No. 15 Squadron, Royal Navy Armoured Car Division with a Lanchester, Newhaven Court, *c.* 1914. The bizarre exploits of this unit, commanded by Oliver Locker Lampson of Newhaven Court, are without parallel. They embarked for Russia to fight alongside the armies of the Czar against the Bolsheviks and went on to fight in the Middle East. Several members of the squadron were recruited from the Cromer area.

Eastern Counties Omnibus Company, Cromer depot, Second World War. The bus company participated in a wartime effort to save petrol by successfully converting some of its fleet to producer gas which was made from coal. Here the crew are maintaining the Tilling producer gas plant, carried on a trailer. Left to right: -?-, garage foreman Bales (kneeling), George Aldiss (on the compressor), Billy Amis, John Long, ? Hurrell.

Section Five

THE HOLIDAY TRADE

The little fishing village was transformed by the holiday trade. Holidaymakers were the driving force that brought a rail connection, new businesses, hotels and boarding houses – and new estates to house the growing population.

Cromer, possibly late 1840s. One of the oldest photographs, the original print was made by the salted paper process from a paper negative. Careful examination of the background shows that the Hotel de Paris had not yet been extended upwards (as it was in 1864) and Albert House had not been built (that happened in 1851). Behind the crab boat, Beach House has only two storeys.

East Beach, 1840s. Dark figures are promenading along the strand, and the bathing machines are drawn to the water's edge. On the cliff top, in the distance, is the shadowy silhouette of the old coal-fired lighthouse that slipped over the edge in 1866.

A lithograph by I.M. Johnson, *c.* 1830. Compare this with the top photograph on the previous page. Cromer's picturesque scenery and fishermen attracted many artists. Thomas Randell's Warm Seawater Baths were on wooden stilts on the beach (right centre with hipped roof). The structure, erected in about the 1820s, was so badly damaged by the storm of 1837 that he took his business to Jetty Street.

The Bath House, 1875. Simeon Simons opened his hot and cold seawater baths in 1814 in a building at the base of the cliff. It was devastated by a storm in 1837 and a man was washed away while trying to rescue furniture. It was rebuilt in 1838 and extended in 1872, when it became an hotel.

The beach, 1880s. These were the days before the Cromer Urban District Council began to curb the activities of the beach tradesmen. Joshua Jacobs had a thriving business in the 1880s and thought he would increase his income with a little advertising on the side of his bathing machines. The Council strongly objected to this and he had to black out the writing. The tented structure on the right is Mr Baldwin's tea tent. It did a flourishing business, despite the Act of Parliament of 1845 that forebade it.

The curious structure in the foreground is illuminated by the following extract from a notebook of Thomas Fowell Buxton, written in 1903: 'There was a tradition in my early life that in the war with Napoleon a French privateer had been sighted off Cromer and that a number of fishing smacks, each armed with a small gun, had gone out and captured her. This was what was told me by my parents. I was also told that the gun used as a post at the top of Gangway and still there [it is also still there in 1995] was taken out of the privateer. When I was a boy (say 1825–35) our gardener (Bowman) used to clip the hedges with a cutlass which . . . I always believed . . . came out of the privateer.

'The captured ship itself was filled with stones and concrete and was embedded in the cliff by the bottom of the gangway as a breakwater to protect the gangway from being washed away in high tides. I can remember when a considerable quantity of the side timbers and the deck remained.'

Sir Thomas Fowell Buxton MP was a philanthropist and fervent anti-slavery campaigner in the early nineteenth century. He lived at Colne House, Cromer.

View of East Beach from the Crescent, *c.* 1894–7. With the exception of the pier that replaced the jetty and the new promenade and seawall, built in 1900, the sea front at Cromer remains almost unaltered.

Three schoolboys messing around near the West Gangway or the Melbourne Slope, 1898. Up the slope are the crab boats of the West Beach fishermen. The white boat near the top of the slope is a hoveller. These were originally used for salvaging wrecks ('hovells') but were also used for fishing. Crab pots and their 'tows' (ropes and floats) are lined up on the slope and handrail. Note that the West Promenade had yet to be built.

Mr John Kettle's goat carts for hire, East Beach, 1892. A fisherman's son in his gansey and boots is in charge of the one on the left. While a little boy digs a hole in the sand, his mother appears to be catching up with some sewing. John Kettle was a greengrocer and hired donkeys as well as goats.

Children playing in the surf, East Beach, 1890. In the background are fishermen and their crab boats, and people are emerging from the bathing machines drawn down to the water's edge. The Hotel de Paris (the tallest building above the cluster of bathing huts) was extended upwards in 1864 and enlarged in 1894 (see p. 62).

A family picnic, Lion's Mouth, Felbrigg Woods, 23 August 1892. Unfortunately we do not know the name of this well-to-do family, but they have cake from Mr Beeze's bakery in High Street, Cromer, tea from china cups and comfort provided by the cushions that were probably taken from their carriage.

The Hotel de Paris, 1891. Originally Lord Suffield's summer residence, it became a hotel in 1830, when Pierre le Francois took it over. On the left is the Lower Tucker's Hotel which was an annexe of the Tucker's Hotel (see p. 46). The Empress Elizabeth of Austria stayed in the Lower Tucker's Hotel in 1887.

Alex Jarvis, the proprietor, had the Hotel de Paris enlarged and completely remodelled by George Skipper, the Norwich architect, in 1894. At the same time they constructed the zigzag path we know today. This is probably the opening of the completed scheme.

East Beach, *c.* 1894–7. The domes of the Hotel de Paris rise over the jetty and, to its left, are the high roofs of the Hotel Metropole. The bathing machines are lined up at the back of the beach and a horse is ready to pull one down to the water's edge. The pleasure craft *Agnes Etta* (see p. 30) is ready to take visitors for a trip.

'After the last bathe', 3 September 1892. A well-to-do but unidentified family on the West Beach comes to the end of another holiday. They preferred to use a tent instead of the bathing machines.

East Beach, 1898. This was in the brief period before the pier was built to replace the old jetty. Women's popular dress for the beach was a high-collared blouse, bow tie and dark skirt. Chairs were wooden slatted on a steel frame, as the deck-chair had not quite arrived at Cromer. Two extremely elegant, and doubtless very wealthy, ladies survey the scene but decline to join in the fun.

Marlborough House, 1891. This began life as a relatively modest corner plot and developed into the large and busy Marlborough Hotel. The latter was owned by F.W. Rogers who also owned the first motor car in Cromer. It is seen below in the late 1890s, before the large ballroom and the dining-room were built on the far right. During the Second World War it was occupied by troops and so extensively damaged that E.G. Gowing, who owned it then, could not reopen. The Jessop brothers bought it and demolished it; the site has variously been used for a petrol station, garage, art gallery and aquarium.

Grand Hotel, 1891. In the 1890s Cromer grew westwards rapidly on land released from the Cromer Hall estate. Here the Grand Hotel, newly opened in 1891, was the lead development of the area west of the centre which contains most of the small hotels and guest-houses. Fire seriously damaged the Grand in April 1969 and it was replaced by the much less grand Albany Flats.

The Royal Links Hotel, *c.* 1900. This was built in 1894 by a consortium of businessmen to take advantage of the Royal Cromer Golf Club nearby and hideously dominated the skyline of the Lighthouse Hills. Edward VII, when he was Prince of Wales, was a keen golfer and stayed here frequently. It burned down in 1949.

The launch of new lifeboat *Louisa Heartwell*, Tuesday 9 September 1902. Under coxswain James Harrison, and later Henry Blogg, the *Louisa Heartwell* did sterling service until replaced by a motor lifeboat in 1923.

Cromer regatta, 1898. The bathing machine attendant and a boy on the horse are watching the lifeboat and a flotilla of crab boats take part.

Cromer Children's Special Service Mission (CSSM), Doctor's Steps, 1898. The mission continues today under the title of the Scripture Union Beach Mission. The photograph was rescued from obscurity: it was found at the back of an old picture.

West Beach. The natural ponding of the tide within the horse-shoe pond was a great resource for paddlers and model yacht sailors before the Second World War.

Building the pier and new promenade, 1900.

Official opening of the new pier, 8 June 1901. Here the crowd is gathering expectantly at the gates.

The Redcoats, 1907. They played at the end of the pier, and there were also regular band concerts. In 1910 the bandstand was developed into the Pavilion Theatre, and shows and concerts have continued to be performed to the present day. Cromer boasts the last remaining genuine 'end of the pier' show in Britain.

Cromer Pier, 1930s. This was its most attractive period. The concert party playing in the Pavilion Theatre was the West End Revellers.

West Beach, *c.* 1935. Chinese parasols, striped woollen bathing costumes, canvas deck-chairs, sun shades, spotted dresses and the first two-piece swimsuit mingle with the last remnants of the bathing machines, now relegated to changing cubicles well back from the sea.

Gordon House, *c*. 1920. Built in 1885, together with the nineteen houses on Meadow Terrace, West Street, it was a boarding house until the First World War. It then became the YMCA Holiday Home. In recent years it was the showrooms of the Eastern Gas Board which closed in 1993.

Section Six

'POPPYLAND'

Centred on Overstrand and Sidestrand near Cromer, 'Poppyland' symbolized the romance of the East Coast – a peaceful haven where jaded urbanites could 'come and be lazy on Cromer Cliffs'. This is Louie Jermy in her 'Poppyland' costume (see p. 78) at the gate of her cottage in Tower Lane, Sidestrand, in the 1920s.

Clement Scott, author, poet and dramatic critic for the *Daily Telegraph*, who through his writings immortalized 'Poppyland'. Below is a recreation of his first meeting with Louie Jermy, miller Alfred Jermy's daughter, at the gate of the Mill House, Sidestrand. His 'Poppyland Papers', describing the East Coast scenery, were published in 1885. He fell in love with Poppyland, though his relationship with Louie apparently remained platonic, and he returned every year until his death in 1904. Many literary and fashionable people from London followed Scott to 'Poppyland', and this boosted Cromer's reputation as a seaside resort.

Louie Jermy, *c*. 1885. Known as the 'Miller's Daughter', 'Maid of the Mill' or 'Louie of the Blackberry Puddings', she became a minor celebrity and was befriended and patronized by the literati of the London stage. Among her guests were the poet Algernon Charles Swinburne and his friend Watts Dunton, satirist George Sims, actors Henry Irving, Wilson Barrett and Nellie Bonser, Beerbohm Tree and many others.

Clement Scott's poem 'The Garden of Sleep' (see opposite) became a popular song when it was set to music by Isidore de Lara. This plagiarization was written soon after the tower had fallen in 1916.

Poppyland Bouquet was manufactured in the early 1900s by Daniel Davison, a retail chemist, local councillor and amateur photographer.

The tower of St Michael's Church, Sidestrand, 1880s. It remained on the cliff top when the church was moved inland in 1881, stone by stone, to avoid its falling into the sea. Trinity House insisted that the tower be left standing as it was an important seamark. The new church is visible in the background. The tower's poignant image, surrounded by its graveyard and, beyond that, cornfields rich with poppies, inspired 'The Garden of Sleep' and many other pieces by Clement Scott. The tower fell down the cliff in 1916.

The fame of 'The Garden of Sleep' and 'Poppyland', on the doorstep of Cromer, inspired books and music. This cover for a piece of sheet music is graced by a portrait of the young Louie Jermy, in a most evocative piece of graphic design.

Part of Lord and Lady Battersea's Pleasaunce, *c.* 1930. One of many large houses built in the late Victorian and Edwardian eras, such houses earned Overstrand the title 'the village of millionaires'. Pleasaunce, like several others here, was designed by Edwin Lutyens; the beautiful gardens were by Cyril Flower (that is Lord Battersea) himself.

Harbord Road, Overstrand, 1890s. Lord Suffield owned the land at the time and Harbord was his family name.

The Old Black Mill, Sidestrand, 1880s. The miller, Alfred Jermy, is standing beside it. He lived at the Mill House nearby with his daughter Louie (see p. 75).

The Mill House and Old Black Mill, Sidestrand, 1880s. Close to the Cromer to Trimingham road it looks as Clement Scott and others would have known it.

In 1918 Louie was evicted from the mill house when her landlord disapproved of the more Bohemian of her guests. She retired to a nearby cottage in Tower Lane but still welcomed visitors, especially theatrical friends. In old age she was often to be seen around Cromer pushing a pram and gathering odd items which she hoarded in her shed.

Rampant cliff erosion, Sidestrand, February 1938. Louie Jermy's cottage, where she died in 1934, is on the right. It finally succumbed to the erosion in 1972.

Beck Hythe, 1880s. This was the old name for the seaward part of Overstrand. In the centre is a tunnel (detail below) constructed from brick and flint. It was built by James Craske so that boats, gear and goods could get from the beach to the cliff top. It proved to be a folly as it was cut into soft glacial boulderclay, and has long since eroded away.

An optimistic 1930s advert for a doomed hotel as cliff erosion edges ever nearer. The hotel, like many others in the area at this time, caught fire and was gutted (below) in 1949.

Overstrand, 1890s. The ruined medieval church of St Martin's was replaced by Christ Church in 1867. Today, however, St Martin's has been restored and its Victorian replacement has been demolished.

Northrepps Cottage, 1880s. This picturesque residence, built for Bartlett Gurney in 1793, was a popular beauty spot. It was the home of Anna Gurney and Sarah Buxton in the early nineteenth century. They began a school for the children of the Overstrand fishermen in the belfry of the ruined church. When the real school was built in 1830 it retained the name of the Belfry School.

Sir Samuel Hoare of Sidestrand Hall (centre back) and his brother (left) with local agricultural workers at the North Walsham and Aylsham Agricultural Association annual show, September 1914.

An unknown Sidestrander, photographed in the grounds of Sidestrand Hall, *c.* 1900.

Mr Balls of Sidestrand, in typical dress of an elderly agricultural worker, *c.* 1900. He wears a chummy hat, jacket and corduroy trousers. His jaw is bearded although his face is shaven and very sun-tanned.

Billy (left) and 'Terrible' Cork, Overstrand fishermen, display an impressive squid, caught in 1938.

Section Seven

SHOPPING

Church Street, Cromer, 1902.

Church Square, after Warwick House had been rebuilt in 1898. The street is double its previous width. From the extreme right: Warwick House (wines and spirits), Hanover House (London Buffet Co. and Rust's shoe shop), Mickleborough House (Randall's ironmongers and Limmers' estate agents), Thurgarton Dairies.

Jetty Street and High Street, 1901. Between the two is Imperial House, occupied by James Curtis, greengrocer and ale and stout merchant. On the left is Rust's frontage, see pp. 90–1.

Half past twelve by the church clock on a summer's day in High Street, Cromer, 1890s. Boxes stand outside the tradesmen's entrance of the Hotel de Paris. Up the street, people are shopping for hats, shoes and Mr Beeze's fresh baked bread and cakes.

Rust's grocery and drapery shop in High Street, 1895. Benjamin Rust established his first Cromer shop in 1780, and until recent years this was the oldest and most successful business in the town. Warwick House on the left was the millinery department.

Interior of Rust's millinery department, 1909.

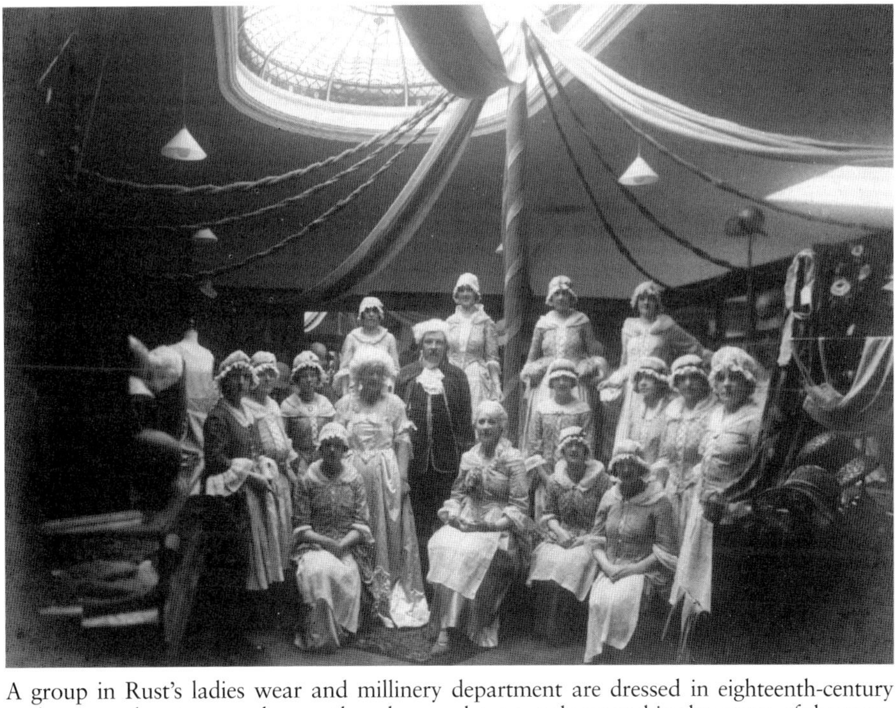

A group in Rust's ladies wear and millinery department are dressed in eighteenth-century mob caps and costume and are gathered around a maypole erected in the centre of the store. The hats for sale suggest this was taken in the 1920s, but on what occasion is not known.

Mr Jimmy Grimble the scribbler for Mr Parker the butcher, 1905. Many customers had accounts with tradesmen and the scribbler kept meticulous accounts in the Day Books and Ledgers.

A wet afternoon for shopping in West Street, with unmetalled roads and pavements of flint beach pebbles, 1890. Churchyard and Sons' West End Supply Stores offered china, glass and earthenware. Avon House in the centre distance was a school for young ladies.

R.A. Clarke's butcher's shop, in Algar House, Church Street, *c.* 1900. His tiny lock-up on this site appears on page 10. The bearded man in the left of the doorway is R.A. Clarke.

Robert Nockels' Royal Fish Stores, Osborne House, New Street, 1900. It has now sadly declined to an amusement arcade – the 'Fun Palace'.

Mr Bancalori, the 'Hokey ice' man walking his carved and highly painted cart along Church Street in 1898. His cry was 'Everybody likes it, it's so nice!' The shops in the background were bombed or demolished after the Second World War.

East House, owned in the 1930s by Tommy Clarke, was one of the most charming properties in Cromer. In 1942 a bomb fell on it and his sister was killed. The house was named after East Street – the old name for part of Church Street. Now it is the site of the Henry Blogg memorial garden and shelter.

Jetty Street, late 1890s. It was usual for the congregation to turn out of church on Sunday mornings and promenade down Jetty Street to the sea. The jettied bay windows were something of a feature in parts of Cromer, and afforded the occupants a privileged view of the sea.

Garden Street, *c.* 1870. On the right is Will Lake's corn chandlery. Next door was John Clarke, hairdresser. The next cottage, which still stands today, was at one time John Cox's, fisherman and fishmonger. Half-way down is Page's drapery and grocery store in London House. Beyond is the flint wall of Hanover House's garden, now a car park.

Garden Street, 1891. On the right Sidney Mutimer's store advertises fancy and plain dress materials at the lowest prices, and he has rolls of linoleum standing on the pavement. Some of the houses on the left side were destroyed by German bombing in July 1942; 'Pimpo' Davies was killed during the attack.

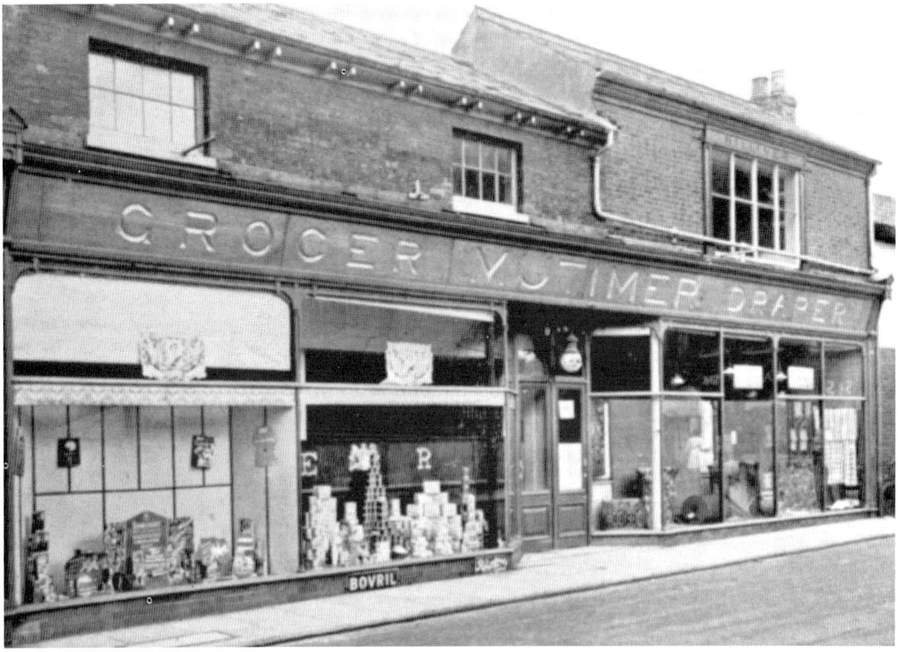

Mutimer's grocery store in Garden Street. They also occupied the building next door, now the Indoor Market. Here the shop is all dressed up to celebrate the coronation of Queen Elizabeth II on 2 June 1953. When three fishermen were drowned on the 5th all the decorations were taken down and the town went into mourning.

Freddie Wells (centre) of Cross Street, *c.* 1930, standing outside his fruit and vegetable stall in Garden Street, which he opened after demobilization following the First World War. The site is now the Women's Institute Hall.

Edward Troller's Cheap Fruit Stores and A.A. Beck's Central Cycle Stores were in the Narrows of Church Street. Mr Troller is the largest chap holding a bicycle. In July 1914 he opened the Regal Cinema in Hans Place, which is still going strong.

Corner of the Narrows, Church Street and Garden Street, 1963. On the corner is the Workers' Cafe, now demolished along with many other properties, in the widening of the street. It is amazing to recall that there was two-way traffic in the Narrows.

Section Eight

THE COMMUNITY

The wedding of Charles Balls and Irene Woodhouse, 1916. The group is gathered in the yard off Chapel Street behind Charles' parents' cottage.

An embarrassing incident: the road menders at work in Church Street, 20 May 1910. This photograph was an indictment against the Cromer UDC for their blatant disregard of a royal proclamation. There was to be a day of general mourning for the late King Edward VII. The Council had in fact issued a precept requesting that the proclamation will be loyally obeyed by the Inhabitants in all Trades, Licensed houses and Businesses. Several tradesmen are among the indignant onlookers.

Domestic staff of Cromer Hall, 1889. So far the following have been identified: back row, fifth from left, Wilcox the butler; third from right, Mr Robin the coachman; right, possibly John William Sparrow the gardener. Front row, left, Fanny Gregory; fourth from left, Thomas William Shingles (1867–1953), who later became estate manager. Fanny Gregory was a servant, and later married the gardener, John Sparrow.

The coach of Marlborough House on Hall Road, 1890s.

The staff of the Cromer Steam Laundry in Cross Street, 1890s. Built in a residential street, the business grew with the holiday trade. In 1913 neighbours complained to the Council about the noise from new machinery, excessive hours (7 a.m. to 9 p.m.) and smoke from the 30 ft chimney.

The funeral cortège of the Maharajah of Cooch Behar climbs the Norwich road to the High station in 1904. A special train took his body to London for cremation. He owned Tudor House, the first house to be built in Cliff Avenue. The Prince of Wales was a frequent visitor there and his Feathers still adorn the fanlight over the door.

Mr and Mrs Risebrow, seen here on their sixty-ninth wedding anniversary in 1908. When this was taken they were ninety and eighty-seven respectively.

The political power in Cromer, *c.* 1910. A posse of well-known dignitaries, who served on the Cromer Urban District Council and Foreshore Commissioners, inspecting the waterworks.

Staff of Girling and Smith's the builders in Cross Street, 1911. They also had a workforce of ninety journeymen. Many firms did very well during the building boom of the 1890s and early 1900s.

Pupils and teachers of Northrepps village school, *c.* 1900.

A pupil on his way to Cross Street Junior School, pre-First World War. The Board School, as it was known, was controversial when it was built in 1894, because of the extravagant quality of the workmanship.

Boy Scouts' tea, possibly at the Vicarage Church Rooms, *c.* 1912. Those present include Tom Pank (front left), 'Carrots' Holdon, Cyril 'Six-a-Side' Sidle, Mrs Parker (Andrew's mother), the Revd Mr Hamilton, Andrew Parker (butcher), Nora Parker (Andrew's sister), ? Ward, Ethel ? (Tucker's Hotel House), ? Swann, Donald (Duck's brother), Jack Danhar (?), 'Sailor' Allen, Harry Chadwick (front right).

Well-bred young ladies from Oakley School, *c.* 1907–13. This private school had several addresses at large houses around Cromer.

The gang of workmen who laid the Prince of Wales Road new sewer. Third from the left on the second row is Lal Thurston, who had something of a reputation for poaching.

Cromer Post Office staff in the yard of the telephone exchange, 1937. Back row, left to right: Bob Spruce, Mr Miller, Mr Greenaway, Bob (?) Amis, Mr Jarvis (?), Steven Coleman. Third row: -?-, Ruth Allen (now Mrs Eales) Henry Wells, Mr Lewis, Mr Trollope (?), -?-, -?-, Miss Harvey, (now Mrs Howell), Miss James, -?-, George Gray, -?-, -?-, Miss Joyce Ling, Miss Molly Avery, Miss Eileen Abbs. Second row: Bob Bristow, Mr Sharman, Miss Joan Ling, Billy Balls, Mr Clarke, Mr Whitworth, Mr John Whiting, Miss Horsley, Miss Ryder, Miss Rump, Bob Hill, Mr Savage. Front row, seated on ground: Billy West, Cyril Mills, Austin Fisher, Cecil Durrant, Colin Spruce, George Sargent.

Cromer Fire Brigade led by Theo Randall (third from left) at a Carnival, probably 1930s. Some of the crew are dressed as bride and bridesmaids with a 'vicar' on horseback (E.H. Harrison); also firemen Jack Danaher (sixth from left), ? Smith (seventh from left) and Picton Hastings (far right, with accordion).

Popular town crier, toastmaster and master of ceremonies Alfie Howard, 1963. Alfie came from Brixham in London on his scooter and 'adopted' Cromer every season from 1959 to the mid-1960s, almost single-handedly organizing events and entertainments of all kinds around the resort.

Cromer Fire Brigade with their engine, soon after formation in 1880. Edward Raven Priest was the Superintendent (standing by rear wheel).

Steaming up the Merryweather fire engine on W.G. Sandford's ground behind Fern House, 1890s.

Beef Meadow, opposite Cromer Hall, was the first football field. This fancy dress match was played in 1912, between the Cromer Shop Assistants and the Warehousemen. Left to right: Billy Atkins, Victor Gregory, -?-, Charlie Maddison, Albert Amis, Cecil Clarke, Jimmy Humphries (behind), Cecil Lamb, -?-, Fred Cox, Gordon Lubbock (behind), Cecil Blythe, -?-, Stanley Jefferies, -?-, -?-, Stanley Lawrence, R.F. Stevens, Gerald Stibbons, Dick Lawrence, -?-, Billy Jacobs (seated), 'Carrots' Holden, Frank Griffin (seated).

First football match at Cabbell Park, home of Cromer FC, September 1922. Norfolk County v. Cromer. Standing: W. Baker, 'Bussey' Allen, Henry Chadwick, Cecil Green, 'Jockey' Reynolds, Tom Durrant, Syd Leggett, Jim Millington, Mr Emms. Seated: Stephen Allen, George Baker, 'Ducky' Swann, 'Rooshy' Kirby, 'Winkle' Abbs, Theo Randall.

Jack Bryant in his record shop on the corner of Church Street and Bond Street, 1965. Alan Smethurst, below, is the Singing Postman from Sheringham ('Ha yer got a light, bor?') making a guest appearance at the shop in 1965. He is being greeted by local printer Ted Cheverton, who has popped round from his works in Bond Street.

Staff of Cromer Hospital, 1933. Drs Vaughan, Colvin Smith, Burton and Fawkes are in the front row, while Dr Miller is standing at the centre. Sadly none of the nurses' names are recorded.

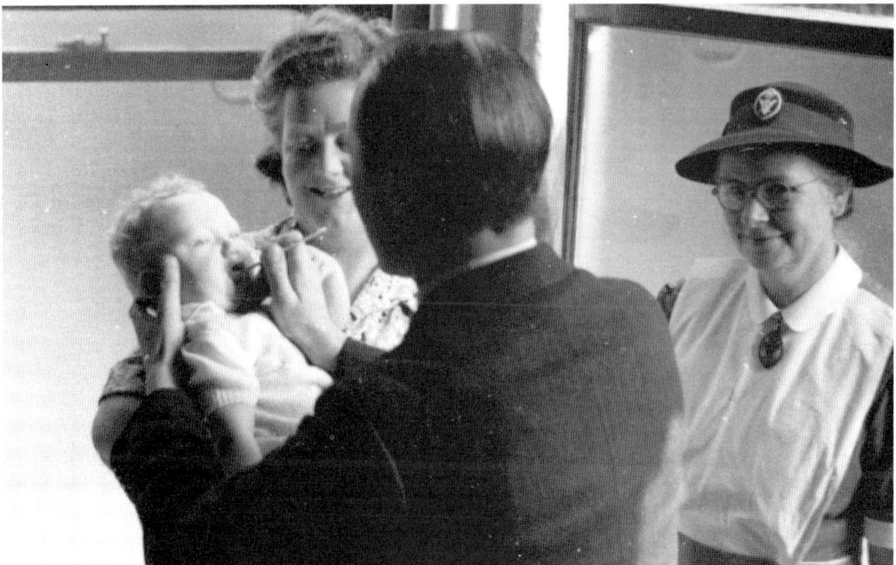

Dr Donald Vaughan and Queen's Nurse Elizabeth Woodard, District Nurse (right) and midwife 1927–60, who during their long careers delivered and treated most of the children of Cromer.

Cromer Choral Society evening concert, 17 May 1906. There is still a strong tradition of amateur dramatic and musical talent in North Norfolk.

Section Nine

THE RUNTONS

East Runton common, c. *1900. 'The Runtons, West and East, form one parish, and are prettily situated on the coast between Sheringham and Cromer. The place has developed rapidly in recent years, and bids fair ere long to prove a serious rival to its larger neighbours on either hand.'*
Ward Lock's Illustrated Guide Book to Cromer and District, *1923–4.*

Crab boats at East Runton Gap, late nineteenth century. Nowadays the modern boats are bigger, with heavy engines, and they rest on trailers. The beach here can be very soft and tracked vehicles are used to launch and recover boats in preference to conventional tractors.

Woodhill, East Runton, *c.* 1905. Before the First World War a film company used this location for 'An Englishman's Home' by William Le Quex. In the film the Germans were shown landing here – a story that almost came true. The cottage fell into the sea in 1966.

The pond on East Runton Lower Common, August 1892. Surrounding the common are some gorgeous seventeenth- to nineteenth-century flint cottages, now supplemented by more modern houses. The village retains much more of its original atmosphere than neighbouring West Runton.

East Runton Mill, late nineteenth century. James Kemp was miller. At one time the mill was owned by Walter de la Mare, the poet.

High Street, East Runton, *c.* 1925.

The Fishing Boat and other properties in the High Street have changed little since the 1950s.

West Runton Golf Course, 1916. The attractive wooded slopes and sandy ground make this an ideal place for a golf course. Other amenities include a convenient station and the comfortable Runton Link Hotel.

A peaceful scene near the railway bridge, West Runton, 1890s. An elderly couple are taking a stroll up Sandy Lane. Beside the road is a typical pair (yes, a pair) of Norfolk cottages of flint and brick under a pantile roof. The ponies are grazing in the fields and a woman hangs out the washing. Old railway carriages are used as serviceable sheds. The cut hay is drying in small stacks. In the distance is the church of the Holy Trinity. West Runton was swollen by residential growth to a much greater extent than its neighbour East Runton.

Section Ten

SUBURBAN GROWTH

A postman on his rounds, Norwich Road, Cromer, c. *1888. 'Behold Cromer Now! Its new hotels springing up in every possible direction . . . with its acres and acres of red houses dotted over valley and hill, with its holiday hamlet of Overstrand . . . and with the spirit of advance stirring all over Poppyland as far as Mundesley on the "Garden of Sleep" side and further than Runton and Sheringham on the other.' Clement Scott,* Daily Telegraph, *August 1896.*

Hans Place (formerly the Loke), 1888. Compare this with the picture on p. 10 and you will appreciate how much Cromer changed in the latter part of the nineteenth century.

Vicarage Road, *c.* 1900. Development spread up the Norwich Road on land formerly belonging to the Cromer Hall estate.

Cabbell Road, *c.* 1900. Two large land sales in 1890 and 1891 sold off all the land between Prince of Wales Road and the Beach Station for speculative development. This area has a high concentration of small hotels and guest-houses.

The Meadow, *c.* 1890. These were the spacious family homes of, for example, stockbrokers, bank managers, teachers, and with room for servants. Compton Mackenzie stayed in the first house as a child. In those days it was called Prospect Villa.

Norwich Road from the corner of St Mary's Road, 1895. There are no houses at all on the east side of the road. The road is only gravel and there is no pavement on the west side.

Northern and Southern Bungalows were built as semi-detached properties and looked very attractive in 1898. They were occupied for many years by Sutherland House School before it moved to The Warren on Overstrand Road.

Construction of houses in Beach Road, *c.* 1904. The carpenters are fitting the windows. The scaffolding is made of wooden poles lashed together, and there are no safety rails.

A party of motorists is seen off from Miss Anna Nockels' apartments at Brockley House, Mount Street, 1920s. To the left was Randall's (watch and clock makers, electricians, wireless accessories and electric light installation) and to the right, the Cromer Gas Company showrooms.

Mill Lane (or Mill Road as it is known now) from an Edwardian postcard, *c.* 1910. The first gas works is up the hill on the right. This is probably the site of the old windmill that gave the street its name.

Station Road, Suffield Park, early 1900s. This was a speculative development on Lord Suffield's estate that linked the centre of town with the site of the Cromer High station.

Cromer Hospital, 1930s. Lady Constance Battersea's legacy provided the money to build Cromer Hospital, which opened in 1932.

The extension of Woolworth's, Church Street, in 1963. The town lost a great deal of character when the flint-and-pantile cottages on both sides of the street were demolished during the widening of the Narrows. The replacement shops are dreary beyond description.

Acknowledgements

Almost all the pictures in this volume are from the collections of the Cromer Museum, which is part of the Norfolk Museums Service. Many images come from the Cyril Crawford Holden collection, which we acquired in 1981. I would like to express my thanks to the many people and organizations who over the years have contributed to the Cromer Museum collection and to a number of dedicated volunteers, especially Charles and Olive Bainton and Rochelle Mortimer, who have helped to preserve and curate the pictures, sifting through facts, typing, cataloguing and indexing. This has both physically preserved them and made the information accessible to the public through a card index and a computer database.

Thanks to the following for kind permission to use photographs: David E. Twitchett, Richard C. March, John Smith, Fergus Wright. My thanks for help with research on some of the pictures go to Ron Bennett, Bobby Briggs, Richard Davies, David and Libby Facey, Philip Sage, Nigel Digby, Jim Smith, John Cox and Beatty Jonas.

BRITAIN IN OLD PHOTOGRAPHS

ALDERNEY

Alderney: A Second Selection, *B Bonnard*

BEDFORDSHIRE

Bedfordshire at Work, *N Lutt*

BERKSHIRE

Maidenhead, *M Hayles & D Hedges*
Around Maidenhead, *M Hayles & B Hedges*
Reading, *P Southerton*
Reading: A Second Selection, *P Southerton*
Sandhurst and Crowthorne, *K Dancy*
Around Slough, *J Hunter & K Hunter*
Around Thatcham, *P Allen*
Around Windsor, *B Hedges*

BUCKINGHAMSHIRE

Buckingham and District, *R Cook*
High Wycombe, *R Goodearl*
Around Stony Stratford, *A Lambert*

CHESHIRE

Cheshire Railways, *M Hitches*
Chester, *S Nichols*

CLWYD

Clwyd Railways, *M Hitches*

CLYDESDALE

Clydesdale, *Lesmahagow Parish Historical Association*

CORNWALL

Cornish Coast, *T Bowden*
Falmouth, *P Gilson*
Lower Fal, *P Gilson*
Around Padstow, *M McCarthy*
Around Penzance, *J Holmes*
Penzance and Newlyn, *J Holmes*
Around Truro, *A Lyne*
Upper Fal, *P Gilson*

CUMBERLAND

Cockermouth and District, *J Bernard Bradbury*
Keswick and the Central Lakes, *J Marsh*
Around Penrith, *F Boyd*
Around Whitehaven, *H Fancy*

DERBYSHIRE

Derby, *D Buxton*
Around Matlock, *D Barton*

DEVON

Colyton and Seaton, *T Gosling*
Dawlish and Teignmouth, *G Gosling*
Devon Aerodromes, *K Saunders*
Exeter, *P Thomas*
Exmouth and Budleigh Salterton, *T Gosling*
From Haldon to Mid-Dartmoor, *T Hall*
Honiton and the Otter Valley, *J Yallop*
Around Kingsbridge, *K Tanner*
Around Seaton and Sidmouth, *T Gosling*
Seaton, Axminster and Lyme Regis, *T Gosling*

DORSET

Around Blandford Forum, *B Cox*
Bournemouth, *M Colman*
Bridport and the Bride Valley, *J Burrell & S Humphries*
Dorchester, *T Gosling*
Around Gillingham, *P Crocker*

DURHAM

Darlington, *G Flynn*
Darlington: A Second Selection, *G Flynn*
Durham People, *M Richardson*
Houghton-le-Spring and Hetton-le-Hole, *K Richardson*
Houghton-le-Spring and Hetton-le-Hole: A Second Selection, *K Richardson*
Sunderland, *S Miller & B Bell*
Teesdale, *D Coggins*
Teesdale: A Second Selection, *P Raine*
Weardale, *J Crosby*
Weardale: A Second Selection, *J Crosby*

DYFED

Aberystwyth and North Ceredigion, *Dyfed Cultural Services Dept*
Haverfordwest, *Dyfed Cultural Services Dept*
Upper Tywi Valley, *Dyfed Cultural Services Dept*

ESSEX

Around Grays, *B Evans*

GLOUCESTERSHIRE

Along the Avon from Stratford to Tewkesbury, *J Jeremiah*
Cheltenham: A Second Selection, *R Whiting*
Cheltenham at War, *P Gill*
Cirencester, *J Welsford*
Around Cirencester, *E Cuss & P Griffiths*
Forest, The, *D Mullin*
Gloucester, *J Voyce*
Around Gloucester, *A Sutton*
Gloucester: From the Walwin Collection, *J Voyce*
North Cotswolds, *D Viner*
Severn Vale, *A Sutton*
Stonehouse to Painswick, *A Sutton*
Stroud and the Five Valleys, *S Gardiner & L Padin*
Stroud and the Five Valleys: A Second Selection, *S Gardiner & L Padin*
Stroud's Golden Valley, *S Gardiner & L Padin*
Stroudwater and Thames & Severn Canals, *E Cuss & S Gardiner*
Stroudwater and Thames & Severn Canals: A Second Selection, *E Cuss & S Gardiner*
Tewkesbury and the Vale of Gloucester, *C Hilton*
Thornbury to Berkeley, *J Hudson*
Uley, Dursley and Cam, *A Sutton*
Wotton-under-Edge to Chipping Sodbury, *A Sutton*

GWYNEDD

Anglesey, *M Hitches*
Gwynedd Railways, *M Hitches*
Around Llandudno, *M Hitches*
Vale of Conwy, *M Hitches*

HAMPSHIRE

Gosport, *J Sadden*
Portsmouth, *P Rogers & D Francis*

HEREFORDSHIRE

Herefordshire, *A Sandford*

HERTFORDSHIRE

Barnet, *I Norrie*
Hitchin, *A Fleck*
St Albans, *S Mullins*
Stevenage, *M Appleton*

ISLE OF MAN

The Tourist Trophy, *B Snelling*

ISLE OF WIGHT

Newport, *D Parr*
Around Ryde, *D Parr*

JERSEY

Jersey: A Third Selection, *R Lemprière*

KENT

Bexley, *M Scott*
Broadstairs and St Peter's, *J Whyman*
Bromley, Keston and Hayes, *M Scott*
Canterbury: A Second Selection, *D Butler*
Chatham and Gillingham, *P MacDougall*
Chatham Dockyard, *P MacDougall*
Deal, *J Broady*
Early Broadstairs and St Peter's, *B Wootton*
East Kent at War, *D Collyer*
Eltham, *J Kennett*
Folkestone: A Second Selection, *A Taylor & E Rooney*
Goudhurst to Tenterden, *A Guilmant*
Gravesend, *R Hiscock*
Around Gravesham, *R Hiscock & D Grierson*
Herne Bay, *J Hawkins*
Lympne Airport, *D Collyer*
Maidstone, *I Hales*
Margate, *R Clements*
RAF Hawkinge, *R Humphreys*
RAF Manston, *RAF Manston History Club*
RAF Manston: A Second Selection, *RAF Manston History Club*
Ramsgate and Thanet Life, *D Perkins*
Romney Marsh, *E Carpenter*
Sandwich, *C Wanostrocht*
Around Tonbridge, *C Bell*
Tunbridge Wells, *M Rowlands & I Beavis*
Tunbridge Wells: A Second Selection, *M Rowlands & I Beavis*
Around Whitstable, *C Court*
Wingham, Adisham and Littlebourne, *M Crane*

LANCASHIRE

Around Barrow-in-Furness, *J Garbutt & J Marsh*
Blackpool, *C Rothwell*
Bury, *J Hudson*
Chorley and District, *J Smith*
Fleetwood, *C Rothwell*
Heywood, *J Hudson*
Around Kirkham, *C Rothwell*
Lancashire North of the Sands, *J Garbutt & J Marsh*
Around Lancaster, *S Ashworth*
Lytham St Anne's, *C Rothwell*
North Fylde, *C Rothwell*
Radcliffe, *J Hudson*
Rossendale, *B Moore & N Dunnachie*

LEICESTERSHIRE

Around Ashby-de-la-Zouch, *K Hillier*
Charnwood Forest, *I Keil, W Humphrey & D Wix*
Leicester, *D Burton*
Leicester: A Second Selection, *D Burton*
Melton Mowbray, *T Hickman*
Around Melton Mowbray, *T Hickman*
River Soar, *D Wix, P Shacklock & I Keil*
Rutland, *T Clough*
Vale of Belvoir, *T Hickman*
Around the Welland Valley, *S Mastoris*

LINCOLNSHIRE

Grimsby, *J Tierney*
Around Grimsby, *J Tierney*
Grimsby Docks, *J Tierney*
Lincoln, *D Cuppleditch*

Scunthorpe, *D Taylor*
Skegness, *W Kime*
Around Skegness, *W Kime*

LONDON

Balham and Tooting, *P Loobey*
Crystal Palace, Penge & Anerley, *M Scott*
Greenwich and Woolwich, *K Clark*
Hackney: A Second Selection, *D Mander*
Lewisham and Deptford, *J Coulter*
Lewisham and Deptford: A Second Selection, *J Coulter*
Streatham, *P Loobey*
Around Whetstone and North Finchley, *J Heathfield*
Woolwich, *B Evans*

MONMOUTHSHIRE

Chepstow and the River Wye, *A Rainsbury*
Monmouth and the River Wye, *Monmouth Museum*

NORFOLK

Great Yarmouth, *M Teun*
Norwich, *M Colman*
Wymondham and Attleborough, *P Yaxley*

NORTHAMPTONSHIRE

Around Stony Stratford, *A Lambert*

NOTTINGHAMSHIRE

Arnold and Bestwood, *M Spick*
Arnold and Bestwood: A Second Selection, *M Spick*
Changing Face of Nottingham, *G Oldfield*
Mansfield, *Old Mansfield Society*
Around Newark, *T Warner*
Nottingham: 1944–1974, *D Whitworth*
Sherwood Forest, *D Ottewell*
Victorian Nottingham, *M Payne*

OXFORDSHIRE

Around Abingdon, *P Horn*
Banburyshire, *M Barnett & S Gosling*
Burford, *A Jewell*
Around Didcot and the Hagbournes, *B Lingham*
Garsington, *M Gunther*
Around Henley-on-Thames, *S Ellis*
Oxford: The University, *J Rhodes*
Thame to Watlington, *N Hood*
Around Wallingford, *D Beasley*
Witney, *T Worley*
Around Witney, *C Mitchell*
Witney District, *T Worley*
Around Woodstock, *J Bond*

POWYS

Brecon, *Brecknock Museum*
Welshpool, *E Bredsdorff*

SHROPSHIRE

Shrewsbury, *D Trumper*
Whitchurch to Market Drayton, *M Morris*

SOMERSET

Bath, *J Hudson*
Bridgwater and the River Parrett, *R Fitzhugh*
Bristol, *D Moorcroft & N Campbell-Sharp*
Changing Face of Keynsham, *B Lowe & M Whitehead*
Chard and Ilminster, *G Gosling & F Huddy*
Crewkerne and the Ham Stone Villages, *G Gosling & F Huddy*
Around Keynsham and Saltford, *B Lowe & T Brown*
Midsomer Norton and Radstock, *C Howell*
Somerton, Ilchester and Langport, *G Gosling & F Huddy*
Taunton, *N Chipchase*
Around Taunton, *N Chipchase*
Wells, *C Howell*
Weston-Super-Mare, *S Poole*
Around Weston-Super-Mare, *S Poole*
West Somerset Villages, *K Houghton & L Thomas*

STAFFORDSHIRE

Aldridge, *J Farrow*
Bilston, *E Rees*
Black Country Transport: Aviation, *A Brew*
Around Burton upon Trent, *G Sowerby & R Farman*
Bushbury, *A Chatwin, M Mills & E Rees*
Around Cannock, *M Mills & S Belcher*
Around Leek, *R Poole*
Lichfield, *H Clayton & K Simmons*
Around Pattingham and Wombourne, *M Griffiths, P Leigh & M Mills*
Around Rugeley, *T Randall & J Anslow*
Smethwick, *J Maddison*
Stafford, *J Anslow & T Randall*
Around Stafford, *J Anslow & T Randall*
Stoke-on-Trent, *I Lawley*
Around Tamworth, *R Sulima*
Around Tettenhall and Codsall, *M Mills*
Tipton, Wednesbury and Darlaston, *R Pearson*
Walsall, *D Gilbert & M Lewis*
Wednesbury, *I Bott*
West Bromwich, *R Pearson*

SUFFOLK

Ipswich: A Second Selection, *D Kindred*
Around Ipswich, *D Kindred*
Around Mildenhall, *C Dring*
Southwold to Aldeburgh, *H Phelps*
Around Woodbridge, *H Phelps*

SURREY

Cheam and Belmont, *P Berry*
Croydon, *S Bligh*
Dorking and District, *K Harding*
Around Dorking, *A Jackson*
Around Epsom, *P Berry*
Farnham: A Second Selection, *J Parratt*
Around Haslemere and Hindhead, *T Winter & G Collyer*
Richmond, *Richmond Local History Society*
Sutton, *P Berry*

SUSSEX

Arundel and the Arun Valley, *J Godfrey*
Bishopstone and Seaford, *P Pople & P Berry*
Brighton and Hove, *J Middleton*
Brighton and Hove: A Second Selection, *J Middleton*
Around Crawley, *M Goldsmith*
Hastings, *P Haines*
Hastings: A Second Selection, *P Haines*
Around Haywards Heath, *J Middleton*
Around Heathfield, *A Gillet & B Russell*
Around Heathfield: A Second Selection, *A Gillet & B Russell*
High Weald, *B Harwood*
High Weald: A Second Selection, *B Harwood*
Horsham and District, *T Wales*
Lewes, *J Middleton*
RAF Tangmere, *A Saunders*
Around Rye, *A Dickinson*
Around Worthing, *S White*

WARWICKSHIRE

Along the Avon from Stratford to Tewkesbury, *J Jeremiah*
Bedworth, *J Burton*
Coventry, *D McGrory*
Around Coventry, *D McGrory*
Nuneaton, *S Clews & S Vaughan*
Around Royal Leamington Spa, *J Cameron*
Around Royal Leamington Spa: A Second Selection, *J Cameron*
Around Warwick, *R Booth*

WESTMORLAND

Eden Valley, *J Marsh*
Kendal, *M & P Duff*
South Westmorland Villages, *J Marsh*
Westmorland Lakes, *J Marsh*

WILTSHIRE

Around Amesbury, *P Daniels*
Chippenham and Lacock, *A Wilson & M Wilson*
Around Corsham and Box, *A Wilson & M Wilson*
Around Devizes, *D Buxton*
Around Highworth, *G Tanner*
Around Highworth and Faringdon, *G Tanner*
Around Malmesbury, *A Wilson*
Marlborough: A Second Selection, *P Colman*
Around Melksham, *Melksham and District Historical Association*
Nadder Valley, *R. Sawyer*
Salisbury, *P Saunders*
Salisbury: A Second Selection, *P Daniels*
Salisbury: A Third Selection, *P Daniels*
Around Salisbury, *P Daniels*
Swindon: A Third Selection, *The Swindon Society*
Swindon: A Fourth Selection, *The Swindon Society*
Trowbridge, *M Marshman*
Around Wilton, *P Daniels*
Around Wootton Bassett, Cricklade and Purton, *T Sharp*

WORCESTERSHIRE

Evesham to Bredon, *F Archer*
Around Malvern, *K Smith*
Around Pershore, *M Dowty*
Redditch and the Needle District, *R Saunders*
Redditch: A Second Selection, *R Saunders*
Around Tenbury Wells, *D Green*
Worcester, *M Dowty*
Around Worcester, *R Jones*
Worcester in a Day, *M Dowty*
Worcestershire at Work, *R Jones*

YORKSHIRE

Huddersfield: A Second Selection, *H Wheeler*
Huddersfield: A Third Selection, *H Wheeler*
Leeds Road and Rail, *R Vickers*
Pontefract, *R van Riel*
Scarborough, *D Coggins*
Scarborough's War Years, *R Percy*
Skipton and the Dales, *Friends of the Craven Museum*
Around Skipton-in-Craven, *Friends of the Craven Museum*
Yorkshire Wolds, *I & M Sumner*